P9-DDD-613

HYPATIA

MATHEMATICIAN, INVENTOR, AND PHILOSOPHER

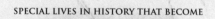

SPECIAL LIVES IN HISTORY THAT BECOME

Signature LIVES

HYPATIA

MATHEMATICIAN, INVENTOR, AND PHILOSOPHER

by Sandy Donovan

Content Adviser: Sophie J.V. Mills, D.Phil.,
Chair and Associate Professor, Classics Department,
University of North Carolina Asheville

Reading Adviser: Rosemary G. Palmer, Ph.D.,
Department of Literacy, College of Education,
Boise State University

Compass Point Books ✦ Minneapolis, Minnesota

Compass Point Books
3109 West 50th Street, #115
Minneapolis, MN 55410

Editor: Anthony Wacholtz
Page Production: Bobbie Nuytten
Photo Researcher: Svetlana Zhurkin
Cartographer: XNR Productions, Inc.
Library Consultant: Kathleen Baxter

Creative Director: Keith Griffin
Editorial Director: Nick Healy
Managing Editor: Catherine Neitge

Library of Congress Cataloging-in-Publication Data
Donovan, Sandra, 1967–
   Hypatia : mathematician, inventor, and philosopher / by Sandy Donovan.
      p. cm.—(Signature lives)
   Includes bibliographical references and index.
   ISBN: 978-0-7565-3760-9 (library binding)
1. Hypatia, d. 415—Juvenile literature. 2. Mathematicians—Egypt—
Biography—Juvenile literature. 3. Women mathematicians—Egypt—
Biography—Juvenile literature. 4. Philosophers—Egypt—Biography—
Juvenile literature. 5. Women philosophers—Egypt—Biography—Juvenile
literature. I. Title. II. Series.
   QA29.H88D66 2008
   510.92—dc22   2007032694

Visit Compass Point Books on the Internet at *www.compasspointbooks.com*
or e-mail your request to *custserv@compasspointbooks.com*

ANCIENT GREECE

The era of ancient Greece began in 1200 B.C. with the fall of Troy in the Trojan War. Soldiers returned to a country mired in famine and economic collapse. It was a time for rebuilding. Greece underwent a political and cultural transformation 400 years after the Trojan War with the transition to independent city-states around 800 B.C. Athens became the hub for developments in architecture, art, science, and philosophy. Ancient Greece entered its golden age, one that would produce the establishment of democracy; the beginnings of university study; great strides in medicine and science; architectural advancements; and the creation of plays and epic poems that are still enjoyed today.

Hypatia

Table of Contents

1 MURDER IN THE STREETS

❧⸙❧

The midday Egyptian sun shone brightly on the streets of Alexandria. It was early spring, the season of Lent, and the city's Christians were preparing for the Easter holiday. As part of the Roman Empire in the year 415, the city of Alexandria was officially Christian, and the season of Lent was one of the holiest times of the year. Christians spent the weeks leading up to this holy day in prayer, personal sacrifice, and fasting—abstaining from food and drink from dawn until dusk. This meant that the city's busy streets were relatively empty on this day.

Hypatia sat in her chariot as the steady clip-clop of her horses' hooves echoed through the winding cobblestone streets. Dressed in the loose-fitting academic robes she always wore, Hypatia looked every part the wise teacher. Her hair hung in long curls down her back, topped by a crown made from the leaves of a laurel tree. She had just delivered a speech in one of the small theaters to some of the highest-ranking city officials. Hypatia's teachings on the history of philosophy and what she called absolute truth were respected by many in the ruling elite.

But her popularity was resented by Christians who considered her teachings a threat to Christianity. Although Christianity was the city's official religion, not all Alexandrians were Christians. The city was home to a thriving Jewish community, as well as to people who still worshipped Greek, Egyptian, and Roman gods. Outbursts of violence between Christians and non-Christians were becoming increasingly frequent.

Alexandria was also home to some of the world's leading thinkers, philosophers, and scientists who

Alexandria was a popular trading center and home to people of many different cultures.

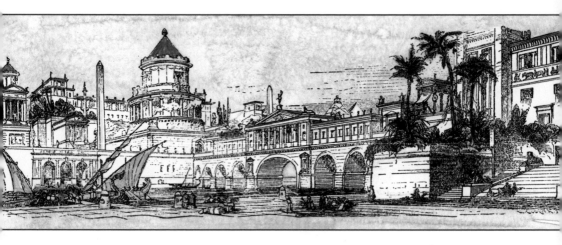

did not believe in any particular gods. Hypatia was the most respected among this group. As a mathematician and scientist, she believed in truths that could be proven by evidence. She did not believe in the teachings of the Christian Bible or the legends of Greek and Egyptian gods.

For decades, she had been recognized as one of the world's leading thinkers, and she had stayed away from Alexandria's ongoing battles between Christians and non-Christians. Still, it saddened her to see her fellow Alexandrians torn apart over religion. As she rode through her beloved city that day, she may have hoped she would soon witness the end of this division. She wanted a world where everyone would see the beauty of scientific and mathematical truths that she had devoted a lifetime to uncovering, studying, and teaching.

Deep in her thoughts, Hypatia probably did not hear the cries of an approaching mob at first. If she did hear their shouts, she probably assumed they were the beginnings of another street fight. But as the mob drew closer, it must have become apparent to the philosopher that she was their target.

Although she was neither a pagan—at the time, the term for a follower of any religion other than Christianity—nor a witch, the crowd could only have been after Hypatia. She was not just the city's best-known mathematician. She was its only famous female resident. At a time when women were only expected to marry and produce children, Hypatia had done neither. Instead of staying quietly in the home, she spent her days teaching, studying, or walking in public and discussing men's topics, such as philosophy, science, and religion. Although she had escaped public wrath for decades, she knew that certain Christians were becoming more and more determined to rid the city of anyone who was not Christian.

As the angry mob surrounded her chariot, her horses were forced to come to a stop. Furiously, arms reached in and grabbed the philosopher. Hands fastened on her white robes, while fists yanked her long hair. Shouting and seething with fury, the mob pulled Hypatia from the chariot.

The crowd's leaders dragged their helpless victim through the streets and into a Christian church called Caesarion. There they ripped off her academic robe, her laurel wreath, and the rest of her clothes. After smashing several of the church's ceramic pots and cups on the stone floor, they stabbed Hypatia repeatedly with the jagged pieces of broken pottery. Once she was dead, they dragged her body through the streets and out of town. At a place called Cinaron, they built a bonfire and burned her body. Although there were no details recorded about this fateful day, some historians believe that this is how the events of Hypatia's death unfolded.

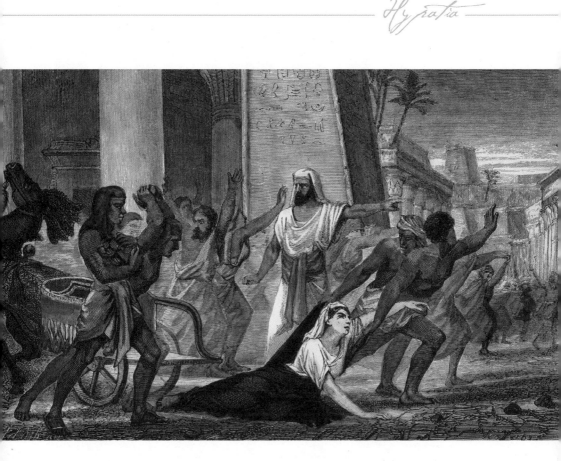

How did the world's leading mathematician and teacher come to such a dramatic end? She may have been murdered for what Christians said was practicing witchcraft and believing in what they thought were false gods. She may have been a random victim of the religious and political violence of her city. Or her murder may have been directed by Alexandria's political leaders to further their own causes. To understand how Hypatia's life ended so tragically, it's important to look at the history and the conflicts of her hometown, Alexandria. ✎

Christians who were furious with pagans targeted Hypatia, who they thought was a pagan.

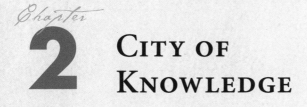

2 CITY OF KNOWLEDGE

❦

Hypatia was born in the late fourth century A.D. to one of the world's leading mathematicians. Her father, Theon, was considered the most distinguished thinker and professor in Alexandria. This magnificent Egyptian city was the Greek center of learning and knowledge. Hypatia was born into the upper class of Alexandria's intellectual society, which was paving the way for creative thought and study.

By the time of Hypatia's birth, Alexandria had been a worldwide hub of learning for many centuries. The city was founded in the fourth century B.C. by the Greek hero Alexander the Great. When Alexander was just 25 years old, he conquered much of the current Middle East. After gaining power in Egypt, he decided to build a new capital city for the region.

He chose Alexandria's location because he admired the natural beauty of the area. The city is nestled between the Mediterranean Sea and Lake Mareotis. A narrow bridge was built to connect the city with Pharos Island in the Mediterranean. Alexander felt this place could become a shipping and trading center because of its access to water. The city was also within sailing distance of the Greek mainland, which is straight across the Mediterranean.

Alexander the Great (356–323 B.C.) conquered much of the known world during his reign as king of Macedonia.

Alexander the Great marked the outline of the city himself. In 323 B.C., Alexandria became Egypt's new capital city. Although it was named after him, Alexander had already moved on to conquer other lands by the time the city was built. When Alexander died, Ptolemy I became the ruler of Greek Egypt. Wanting Alexandria to be the cultural and intellectual capital of the world, Ptolemy founded the Great Library of Alexandria. It was in this library that the famous mathematicians Theon and Hypatia, his daughter, would eventually work.

According to one ancient account of how the library was created, the man assigned to tutor Ptolemy's son had begun collecting books from many parts of the world for the future king. That tutor inspired the building of a library in which to keep them. Built in about 300 B.C., it was also a temple dedicated to the Muses—the Greek goddesses of art, culture, and science. It was named the Museum. The

Although Alexander the Great planned the layout of Alexandria, he died before he was able to return to the completed city.

word *museum* meant "house of the muses," and this museum—the world's first—was a place for worshipping and for learning.

Archaeologists have never uncovered the ruins of the Museum, where Hypatia spent a great deal of her youth. They think it stood in the northeast corner of Alexandria, near the royal palace. From written descriptions of the building, they know it had a large domed dining hall in the middle, with a large terrace for observing the stars. They also know it existed

Alexandria lies on the northern coast of Egypt, which borders the Mediterranean Sea.

Map shows modern boundaries.

Black Sea

Byzantium

Euphrates R.

GREECE ●Troy ●Gordium

Tigris R.

●Athens ●Ephesus
●Sparta ●Miletus

Issus●

●Knossos

Mediterranean Sea

Sidon●
Tyre●

Jerusalem●

Alexandria●

Memphis●

0 |300 miles EGYPT
0 300 kilometers

Nile R.

Red Sea

for at least 700 years, from the days of Ptolemy I in 300 B.C. to Hypatia's lifetime in 400 A.D. During these seven centuries, the Museum and surrounding buildings grew into the largest library in the world, the Great Library of Alexandria.

Ptolemy I sent letters to the leaders and governors he knew, asking them to send books. He collected books written in Latin and Old Persian or other ancient languages and then had each one copied or translated. This involved copying each text word for word with a pen onto parchment or other paper. It took 72 rabbis, or Jewish scholars, to translate the Old Testament of the Bible into Greek.

For several centuries, Alexandria's leaders were immensely proud of the library and worked hard to expand its collection. Sometimes, however, they used ruthless means to obtain books. Rumors flew that any ship entering the port of Alexandria was searched for books, which were confiscated for the library. Another rumor was that visitors to the city were required to surrender any books they might be carrying. These books were translated, then the originals were returned to the owner.

It is estimated that at its peak, the library held more than half a million texts from countries including Assyria, Greece, Persia, Egypt, and India, as well as from the Roman Empire. Books at the time were handwritten rolled scrolls usually made out of papyrus, a local plant. The rolled-up scrolls were stored in pigeonholes with their names printed on leather tags that hung from their ends. The pigeonhole shelves probably lined the wall of a Great Hall next to the domed dining hall. They were probably found in outlying buildings as well.

A simple filing system using pigeonholes stored an estimated 500,000 scrolls in the Great Library.

The Museum was surrounded by beautiful gardens and a zoo filled with exotic animals imported from all corners of the known world. There were also shrines to each of the nine Muses on the museum grounds.

This building was more than just a temple in which to store books. It became the intellectual capital of Egypt and Greece. The Museum was home to the greatest thinkers of the time, including Hypatia and her father. Men who studied philosophy, astronomy, medicine, mathematics, and geometry researched, lectured, and wrote at the Museum. They held classes in several lecture halls throughout the building.

Many of the men probably lived on the Museum grounds. Others lived with their families in other parts of Alexandria but spent their days reading and lecturing at the Museum. In many ways, the Museum was like a modern university.

A "daughter library" called the Serapeum was located at the Temple of Serapis. Archaeologists have uncovered remains of the Serapeum and know exactly where it stood.

Throughout the last centuries of the B.C. era, the Museum and the Great Library remained the center of scientific and philosophical thought in the Greek world. The Ptolemy family ruled Alexandria—and the rest of Egypt—until 30 B.C. Over the three centuries of the Ptolemaic Empire, 15 kings (Ptolemy I through Ptolemy XV) and several queens held the throne.

During this time, Alexandria flourished as the largest city in the world. Life inside the Museum was peaceful and thoughtful, and some of the greatest breakthroughs in science, medicine, and astronomy took place there.

However, the rest of Alexandria was a chaotic place. The Ptolemaic Empire oppressed people with huge taxes, and many unhappy citizens attempted to

Along with the Museum and Serapeum, Alexandria was home to many other famous landmarks. One of them was the Pharos, or lighthouse, which was considered one of the seven wonders of the ancient world.

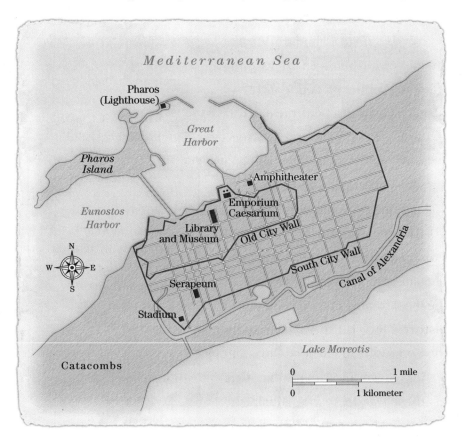

revolt. The Ptolomies could be merciless rulers, often killing enemies who may not have even committed a crime. Within the royal family, scandals were commonplace. There were rumors that several kings had their parents murdered in order to take the throne themselves. Kings' wives were also known to murder their stepchildren to prevent them from taking over.

When Queen Cleopatra VII lost an important battle in 31 B.C., the Roman Empire gained control of Alexandria. By this time, the city was already quite multicultural. There were separate Greek, Egyptian, and Jewish communities within the city, and fighting was common.

After Alexandria fell into Roman control, the city eventually became a major setting for one of the most important events in world history: the birth of Christianity. Some of the earliest Christian leaders lived in Alexandria. One of these leaders was Mark the Evangelist, who was killed—and

Cleopatra VII's reign over Egypt (51–30 B.C.) marked the end of the Ptolemaic dynasty and the beginning of Roman rule over Alexandria and the rest of Egypt. During her life, she co-ruled Egypt with three of her brothers. When the Roman leader, Julius Caesar, arrived in Alexandria, Cleopatra quickly became allies with him. Later, after Caesar was assassinated, Cleopatra formed a long-standing relationship with Marc Antony, one of Caesar's generals. When the pair lost Alexandria in a battle with another Roman leader, Octavian, they both committed suicide. After Cleopatra's death, Alexandria was ruled by the Roman Empire for more than five centuries.

*Christians were
thrown to the
lions in front
of large crowds
in amphithe-
aters across the
Roman Empire.*

later made a saint—because he protested against people worshipping the Greek-Egyptian god Serapis at the Serapeum. The Roman Empire persecuted some of the early Christians for not believing in Roman or Greek gods. In 284 A.D., it was estimated

that tens of thousands of people were killed for being Christians.

When the Roman Empire officially adopted the religion of Christianity, the bloody battles between Christians and pagans persisted. The Museum, which was itself a temple to Greek gods, was embraced by pagans but detested by Christians.

Although learning and research continued at the Museum until late in the fourth century—when Hypatia's father, Theon, was a leading professor there—they were losing much of their popularity by then. The conflict between pagans and Christians would be a major element of Hypatia's life. It would also ultimately lead to her death. ❧

3 THEON'S DAUGHTER

೮౮෩౩౨ಿ

Within the Alexandrian world of cultural and religious conflict, Hypatia's father, Theon, was famous. He remained sheltered from most of the battles over religion. Instead, he was known for his scientific thought. He was a mathematics teacher and an editor of math and astronomy textbooks. Besides teaching at the Museum, Theon was sometimes referred to as the "president" of the Museum, indicating that he was more than a teacher.

Considered brilliant by everyone who knew him, he specialized in making famous scientific writings understandable to readers. He edited a famous mathematics text called *Elements*, which had been written about 600 years earlier by the Greek mathematician Euclid. Theon also wrote about Ptolemy—not the

Euclid (c. 323–283 B.C.), known as the father of geometry, taught mathematics at the Museum.

king of Egypt, but the early Greek astronomer with the same name—whose description of the solar system was widely accepted at the time.

Although historians know much about Theon, not much is known about Hypatia's mother. Even Hypatia's exact date of birth is uncertain. However, since they are fairly certain that she died around 415, and since most descriptions describe her beauty but never mention her growing old, some historians believe she must have died before she was 50. Therefore, they assume that she must have been born around 370. Other people have used science to try to determine her birth year. Scientists know that Theon recorded two complete eclipses—one of the sun and one of the moon—and they have been able to date these events to 364. So they know that Theon was an adult by that year. This leads them to believe that Hypatia was born around then. However, most historians agree this is pretty weak evidence for a birth year. They can only guess that Hypatia was born between 350 and 370.

Little is known about Hypatia's childhood, but it was not a typical girlhood of the time. In an era when most young girls were kept close to home with female relatives, Hypatia learned about the world from her father.

Life in Alexandria was strictly divided by classes then. As a member of the elite intellectual community, Hypatia is likely to have come in contact with the city's political leaders and wealthy business owners but not with the common people. She likely spent

Although Hypatia's father, Theon, is remembered as a great mathematician and astronomer, he was also a poet. In his most famous poem, which he dedicated to the astronomer Ptolemy, he sings the praises of Ptolemy's model of the universe. He writes about the beauty of the starry skies and the perfect world inhabited by the gods that lies beyond the moon and stars.

her days at the Museum, reading and working with her father, listening to him debate issues with colleagues, and attending lectures in the grand auditoriums. Theon taught his daughter math and science, as well as art, literature, and philosophy.

Most historians agree that Hypatia never traveled far from Alexandria, although some believe that she went to Athens to study. Portraits of Hypatia show her wearing a crown made of a laurel wreath that the

Ancient Greeks also used laurel wreaths to honor winning athletes.

Academy of Athens gave its top graduating students each year. The depictions of the beautiful scholar wearing the Athenian laurel led some historians to believe that she studied at Athens. However, the portraits were made long after Hypatia's lifetime, so it is hard to know whether she studied there.

While she was still a young adult, Hypatia learned all she could from her father. She then began her own research of classical mathematical texts. The historian Socrates Scholasticus, who lived about the same time as Hypatia, recorded an early history of Christianity. He wrote:

> *She inherited her father's extraordinarily distinguished nature, and was not satisfied with the training in mathematics that she received from her father, but turned to other learning also in a distinguished way.*

Hypatia not only learned from her father, but she also worked closely with him. She contributed to many of his "Commentaries," or revisions, of older texts. These revisions helped students understand the works of the great Greek mathematicians and scientists who lived centuries earlier. In one of these texts, Theon included a footnote stating that one whole chapter was revised by "my philosopher-daughter Hypatia." In another note, he described

Hypatia as having surpassed his own knowledge. Together they collaborated on several editions of famous mathematical and astronomical texts. While some of the texts they worked on together still exist today, no examples of Hypatia's independent work have survived.

Though they worked closely together, their interests were sometimes different. Theon was interested in the mythical side of Greek culture. Like most early Greeks, he believed that the future could be foretold by listening to "signs" from the planets and living creatures. But Hypatia was more interested in scientific study, in which truths are understood from evidence. Her style of teaching was dialectic, meaning that students learn from a professor through question-and-answer sessions.

Hypatia also experimented in many fields of science and has been credited with inventing machines. Some scholars think that she may have invented two water machines: one to distill water and another to measure the level of water. Most historians agree that she helped invent the plane astrolabe for measuring the positions of the stars, planets, and sun.

> *Historians remain uncertain about what happened to the Great Library's huge collection of books and scrolls. According to one story, when Julius Caesar was living in Alexandria, he lit a massive fire in the harbor to defend against the attack of another Roman general. This fire may have burned down part of the Library and much of its contents.*

Plato (c. 428–348 B.C.) used the dialectic style of teaching at the Academy, a school of philosophy and science he founded in 387 B.C. in Athens.

She also likely helped invent the hydrometer—which determines how much liquid weighs—and the hydroscope, for observing objects under water.

At this time in Alexandria, most of the Christians were uneducated and poor. They did not place much value on learning. But a small group of elite non-Christians took learning seriously and greatly respected intellectuals. All of the academics at the time, except for Hypatia, were men. They wore long, rough-textured robes called academic cloaks

Greek scholarly men, easily identified by their academic cloaks, frequented Alexandria's Great Library.

and spent much of their time researching or writing at the Museum and surrounding libraries. They also delivered public lectures in the city center. This central public gathering spot was a common feature of Greek cities, and crowds often gathered to hear

political proclamations or listen to famous speakers. These crowds were generally male only.

However, as Socrates Scholasticus wrote:

> *Although [Hypatia] was a woman she put on a man's cloak and made her way into the centre of the city and gave to those who wanted to listen public lectures about Plato or Aristotle or about some other philosophers.*

Other historians agree that Hypatia was highly admired by the Alexandrian public. Scholasticus summed up this feeling: "The other citizens understandably were fond of her and accorded her the greatest respect, and the current magistrates of the town always went first to her."

Part of Hypatia's appeal was her sharp mind and intellect, but she was also loved for her polite attitude and her beauty. No images or physical descriptions from Hypatia's time exist today, but throughout history, she has been pictured as looking similar to the Greek goddess Athena, with a classic Greek profile and long flowing curls. Scholasticus wrote that she was "so beautiful to look at that one of her pupils fell in love with her." But Hypatia never married and discouraged any suitors who showed an interest in her. Instead, she concentrated on thinking, writing, and teaching. ॐ

4 PLATONISTS, PAGANS, AND CHRISTIANS

❧⁓❧

As an adult, Hypatia was recognized as the world's leading mathematician. But she was also one of the leading philosophers of her time. Around 400, she became the official head of the Platonic school in Alexandria. The Platonic school was more a group of like-minded philosophers than an actual school. There was no physical school, although many Platonists were associated with the Museum in Alexandria. Although Theon was the head of the Museum, Hypatia taught most of her students in her own home. Among her students were the sons of Alexandria's most influential families, and she taught them all according to her Platonic beliefs.

Platonists—members of the Platonic school—based their philosophy on the teachings of Plato,

Hypatia is thought to be the only woman shown in the painting School of Athens, *created by the famous Renaissance artist Raphael.*

37

the ancient Greek philosopher who lived in Athens in about 400 B.C. Plato was famous for writing *Dialogues*—fictional accounts of his teacher arguing philosophy with a variety of real and fictional characters. Almost 800 years after Plato's lifetime, Hypatia and her fellow Platonists of Alexandria were committed to preserving the philosopher's ideas. The Platonists valued not only Plato's ideas, but also his methods for revealing truth. Hypatia's teaching style of question-and-answer sessions with her students was modeled after the method in *Dialogues*.

Plato's series of Dialogues *covers a range of subjects, including philosophy, math, and logic. Plato himself does not appear in any of the* Dialogues. *However, some are written in first person, with the author in the role of Plato's renowned teacher, Socrates. Today many of the* Dialogues *are still used to teach complicated philosophical concepts.*

Among other things, Plato is remembered for Platonic idealism—the theory that ideas are more real than things, and that things are only a reflection of a higher truth. Hypatia was particularly interested in this idea and used mathematics to illustrate it.

For example, if she would tell her students to imagine they had a pair of sandals, the students knew that the objects were two sandals. If they imagined two people, they knew without counting that it was a pair of people. So the idea of a pair— and the number 2—exists in a more profound, or

real, way than the actual people or sandals do.

Hypatia and other Platonists of her time took this idea even further than Plato did. They believed

To Hypatia, the idea of a pair of people was more of a reality than two actual people.

that behind every thought or object on Earth there existed an even deeper reality, a kind of idea behind all other ideas. Platonists called this the One, and they believed that it was at the center of all human thought and life. Although Plato had mentioned this idea, Hypatia's group of scholars emphasized it much more than he ever had. They believed the One was at the center of their whole philosophy. Because of this new emphasis, historians named this group Neoplatonists, or new Platonists. Neoplatonists also put more emphasis on science and mathematics than Plato and his earlier followers had.

The idea of One and the Christian God had a lot in common. Both were supreme beings who were omniscient (all-knowing) and omnipotent (all-powerful). However, the Neoplatonists were not Christians. Most of them were considered pagans, which meant they either had no religion or they worshipped ancient Greek, Egyptian, or Roman gods. To Christians, either having no religion or worshipping many gods was both anti-Christian.

Hypatia did not seem to worship any gods in particular. Instead, she believed in the power of rational thought and the idea that the laws of nature can be learned from observation and experimentation.

Although Hypatia did not believe that religion held the answers to all questions about nature and the universe, her philosophy was considered to be

Plato's theories on reality and truth were the basis for the Neoplatonists' views and ideas.

religious because it attempted to explain human life. Unlike most religions, it was not heavily based on worship. Instead, Hypatia and other Neoplatonists

Plotinus (center), the founder of Neoplatonism, believed that the material world was not real and that life was merely an illusion.

placed the highest value on scientific thought and reason. They valued the logic and truth they found in mathematics. They did not agree with the Christian practice of accepting views as they are explained in the Bible simply because they are in the Bible.

Hypatia believed in relying on scientific evidence to increase human knowledge. She also believed in Plato's technique of questioning to achieve understanding. As Hypatia explained, "Reserve your right to think, for even to think wrongly is better than not to think at all."

Above all, Hypatia believed firmly in education as a means of identifying truths. At a time when very few girls received formal education, she spoke of the need to teach scientific truth to all children, boys and girls alike. She also warned about the dangers of teaching children myths and fairy tales:

> Fables should be taught as fables, myths as myths, and miracles as poetic fancies. To teach superstitions as truth is a most terrible thing. The mind of a child accepts them, and only through great pain, perhaps even tragedy, can the child be relieved of them.

Hypatia was unimpressed with what she called religious superstition. She once described how she felt "truth" was different from religious beliefs: "Men will fight for superstition as quickly as for the living truth— even more so, since superstition is intangible, you can't get at it to refute it, but truth is a point of view, and so is changeable."

To Christian leaders, these ideas were heretical. They went against the teachings of the Bible, which contained stories that many Christians accepted as truth without scientific evidence.

But the similarities between Hypatia's beliefs and Christianity were obvious to many of her students, even if they were not obvious to most of Alexandria's

Christian leaders. One of her star pupils was a pagan man named Synesius of Cyrene. He learned Neoplatonist ideas, including the idea of One, from Hypatia. But as an adult, he moved to Athens and converted to Christianity, becoming a leading Christian thinker. He believed in the idea of the Trinity, the union of three divine persons—the Father, the Son, and the Holy Spirit—in one God. Historians agree that this idea of the Trinity was in part based on the Neoplatonist idea

The Christian concept of the Trinity includes the Father (God), the Son (Jesus), and the Holy Spirit.

of One. Long after he converted to Christianity, Synesius continued to hold his former teacher in the highest esteem. From his new hometown, he wrote:

> Athens has no longer anything sublime except the country's famous names. Today Egypt has received and cherishes the fruitful wisdom of Hypatia.

Even though many people considered her to be a pagan, Hypatia was not thought of as an actual enemy of the Christian church. It seems that the church left her alone to work and teach through at least the mid-380s, probably because of her extraordinary popularity and modest nature. Although Hypatia held strong ideas about science and the quest for knowledge, she did not look for trouble when tensions were mounting between Christians and pagans in Alexandria. ✆

Hypatia's students, who came from all over Egypt as well as from neighboring countries, were members of the elite class. She taught them privately in her home or held "private" public lectures at theaters in Alexandria. Both she and her students appear to have thought that common people were not capable of understanding the philosophical issues they discussed. The students considered Hypatia their "divine guide" and called the knowledge that she taught them "mysteries."

Chapter

5 CLASH OF SCIENCE AND RELIGION

❧❦❧

For centuries before Hypatia's time, Alexandria was a melting pot of different races and religions. When Hypatia lived there, the city was home to Egyptians, Greeks, and Romans. Christians, Jews, and pagans lived in separate communities. Each religious community had its own places of worship. There were Jewish temples, Christian churches, and pagan temples, such as the Museum and the Serapeum. Sometimes the groups tolerated each other. At other times, fighting and mob violence occurred between Christians and non-Christians, including Jews and pagans. In the late 380s, violence increased throughout the city.

As in the rest of the Roman Empire, the official religion of Alexandria was Christianity. But as a center of learning and philosophy, Alexandria was

After a pagan wedding, it was customary to sacrifice a bull in hopes that the gods would look favorably upon the newly married couple.

home to some of the leading pagan thinkers of the time—including Hypatia. As her popularity as a teacher and public speaker increased, Christian leaders deepened their mistrust of her. They did not like the fact that she did not teach Christian beliefs. They grew concerned that she had such a large following among Alexandrians. Because she was considered the empire's greatest living teacher, even some prominent Christian families sent their sons to learn from her. Making matters even worse, Hypatia made public statements against organized religion:

> All formal ... religions are delusive [able to easily mislead people] and must never be accepted by self-respecting persons as final.

But there was another reason for the suspicions against Hypatia. Besides being considered a pagan, Hypatia had come to symbolize science and mathematics—two topics growing more and more out of favor with the Christian church at the time.

Much mathematical and scientific study at the time centered on astronomy and understanding the universe. Since the beginning of time, people had worked to understand the planets and stars. This came from a desire not only to understand the history of Earth, but also to foretell the future. Almost all religions—including Christianity and paganism—

included stories and theories that explained Earth's position in the universe. They also included explanations of how the future is determined. For example,

Greek astronomers studied the stars from Alexandria's observatories.

many Christians believe the future is determined by God's will.

In the fourth century, astronomers could scientifically foretell things before they happened, such as where planets would be in any given year or when eclipses would take place. To the common people of Alexandria, this knowledge of the future seemed magical, and it made them want to know other things about the future. Most people did not care about when the next eclipse would take place, but they did want to know details about their personal or financial futures.

Some dishonest people took advantage of people's desire for knowledge about the future. Often calling themselves mathematicians or scientists, they claimed they could tell people anything they wanted to know about the future. They set up shops where they gave customers made-up information about future events, giving a bad name to more serious mathematicians and scientists like Hypatia.

So while church leaders had a valid reason to suspect these "pretend" mathematicians, they often did not distinguish them from real mathematicians—they mistrusted all of them. In the mid-300s, priests were forbidden from practicing mathematics. Before long, the Roman Empire passed a law: "No one may consult a soothsayer [fortune-teller] or a mathematician."

The Roman Empire was determined to rid itself of non-Christians. In some cases, it tried to convert pagans gently. For instance, church leaders began to declare new church holidays that fell on the same dates as popular pagan holidays. Christians hoped that this would make it easy for pagans to switch to the Christian church while still celebrating and worshipping at familiar times.

The empire also reacted more harshly to some pagan practices. Throughout the empire, pagan temples and statues were knocked down and burned. In 389, the Roman emperor, Theodosius, passed laws turning all the major pagan holidays into workdays, making it illegal for pagans to worship at certain times.

In 391, Theodosius outlawed blood sacrifices, a common pagan practice in which a goat or a calf was killed to make a god happy. Under the new law, the punishment for performing such a sacrifice was death. Theodosius also decreed that "no one is to go to the sanctuaries, walk through the temples, or raise his eyes to statues created by the labor of man."

Public opposition to mathematicians grew with this persecution of pagans, but Hypatia refused

Theodosius gained military experience as a young man in what are now England and Germany. After a military career, he became emperor of the Roman Empire, located in Constantinople, in 379. After a near-death experience in 380, the new emperor became an extremely devout Christian. In 381, he ordered that all pagan temples and other churches be turned over to the church. Theodosius was the last ruler of a united Roman Empire. When he died in 395, the Roman Empire was split into two parts, the East and the West— each one ruled by one of Theodosius' sons.

Theodosius (center) gave away his niece, Serena, during a Christian wedding.

to be frightened away from her beliefs. She said, "To rule by fettering the mind through fear of punishment in another world is just as base as to use force." Still, Hypatia seemed to live without much personal harassment, probably because of her gentle nature. She remained a symbol of learning, and many Christians were proud to have her representing their city.

But the two homes of Alexandria's Great Library—the Museum and the Serapeum—were prime targets for the growing hatred of paganism. Following Theon's death in the early fifth century, the Museum was no longer an active learning institution. Together with the Serapeum, it now represented the last stronghold of pagan worship.

The exact date of Theon's death is unknown, but historians agree that he lived at least until Hypatia was a grown woman. Many believe he stopped teaching in 391 and died in 405.

Although it was called the "daughter library," the Serapeum temple was an enormous, strikingly beautiful building. Its role as library was secondary to its status as a temple to the Greek-Egyptian god Serapis—the god of both the dead and healing. The temple contained a large statue of Serapis made of metal, wood, and colorful stones, including sapphire, hematite, emerald, and topaz.

Serapis was depicted as having a rich, dark blue body, gold and silver clothing and sandals, and an elaborate headgear with fruit springing from it. The statue had outstretched arms with hands that touched the walls of the main temple. Nearby seats allowed worshippers to sit and meditate on the god.

Ancient Greeks honored their gods, such as the river god, Tiber, by erecting statues.

Outside the temple was a large courtyard that opened onto small houses for priests, priestesses, and visitors. For centuries, visitors came to the temple for an "incubation." During this ritual, a person with an illness or even a nonmedical problem would sleep inside the temple until he or she received a dream that revealed what treatment or solution would solve the problem. Believing that it held such strong powers of healing, pagans held the Serapeum in the highest esteem. ℘

6 DESTRUCTION OF A TEMPLE

⤜✦⤛

On a hot day in 391, Alexandria's central square was crowded with people. The sun beat down on the crowd, which was a mix of the city's residents—men and women, Christians and pagans. Normally at this time of day, women would be home preparing the noon meal and men would be working. But today a long-awaited message from Emperor Theodosius was expected to arrive. Hypatia, who was in her 20s or 30s then, was probably not among the crowd, but she likely knew of the importance of the day. It was rumored that the emperor was going to issue another order having to do with pagan worship.

All of Alexandria knew that the city's archbishop, Theophilus, was determined to eliminate pagan worship from his area. The archbishop was the local

Even though influential religious leader Saint Ambrose, bishop of Milan, rebuked Theodosius for his ruthless acts toward non-Christians, Theodosius continued to act harshly toward them.

Theodosius was the last emperor to rule the entire Roman Empire.

leader of the Christian church. He had authority over anything having to do with the church, including when people should worship and how much money they should give to the church.

For other matters, the archbishop had to consult with the Roman emperor in Constantinople or with the emperor's representative in Alexandria, the local governor. Some people said Theophilus had personally asked the emperor to allow him to burn down all pagan temples. Others said he had asked that all pagans be expelled from the city. Now Theophilus was about to receive his answer. The gathered crowd waited expectantly. What would the emperor decree?

In those days, messages from the emperor were sent by special courier on horseback. The courier rode in a grand procession, surrounded by sword-carrying soldiers as bodyguards. It could take days or even weeks for the party to reach its destination and deliver its message. But often a scout—a faster rider—would gallop ahead to announce the coming arrival of the emperor's messenger.

Early that morning, the scout had arrived in Alexandria, so residents, including Hypatia, knew it would not be long. Suddenly, the crowd bustled with excitement as the messenger drew near. Dressed in an imperial uniform and flanked by soldiers, the messenger approached the parting crowd.

In the square's center, Archbishop Theophilus greeted the emperor's men. The messenger bowed and handed the archbishop a rolled-up scroll containing a letter from Theodosius. After the greeting, the archbishop read the letter, smiled, and handed it to his spokesman.

After the spokesman quieted the crowd, the sea of Alexandrians grew still as they awaited the emperor's words. The middle of the square was packed with Christians, eager to gain more support for their religion. At the edges of the crowd, pagans stood anxiously, worried that they were about to receive disastrous news.

The spokesman's voice boomed through the crowd, declaring that the worship of false gods was forbidden. He also said that the houses of worship, together with the images of false gods, could be destroyed. Moreover, all symbols and idols of false gods could be confiscated, distributed, and sold for precious metals to improve the lives of Alexandria's poorest citizens.

Christians cried out with joy. But the pagans were stunned. What would happen to their beloved temples, the Museum, and the Serapeum? How would they worship? It is not known when Hypatia learned of the decree, but since she had spent much of her time at the Museum, the news was likely upsetting to her.

Some pagans left quietly, but others became angry. One pagan named Olympus began to rally his friends. As the crowd began to disperse from the square, Olympus led his group in a chant, saying that they would die with their gods. Violent fights broke out around the square between Christians and pagans.

Meanwhile, Archbishop Theophilus led a mob of Christians toward the Serapeum. Theophilus marched

Scholars were concerned what would happen to their Great Library after the emperor's decree.

The god Serapis was likely an invention of the Egyptian King Ptolemy I (323–283 B.C.). The god, who represented fertility, combined elements of both Greek and Egyptian mythology. Historians believe that Ptolemy I created Serapis as a way of uniting the Greek and Egyptian residents of Alexandria. Serapis is almost always depicted—either in a painting or a sculpture—wearing a basket for measuring grain on his head. This was a Greek symbol for the land of the dead. The three-headed dog Cerberus, a symbol of the underworld, is usually shown at Serapis' feet. Also commonly shown at his feet is a cobralike head of a serpent, which was an Egyptian symbol for royalty.

at the front of the mob, clutching and waving a Christian cross. Following him were his most trusted monks, wild with religious fervor. Trailing the monks was a large crowd of Christians, eager to see what their leaders would do.

Reaching the temple and the large statue of Serapis, the archbishop and his monks grabbed the large pillars and dislodged one, then another. The crowd cheered, but as the pillars gave way, many of the assembled stood back and began to tremble with fear. Although they were Christians, they still had superstitions about these pagan gods, and they feared Serapis would strike out at those who tried to destroy him.

As a soldier raised a heavy ax against the face of Serapis, the crowd grew nervous. The soldier hesitated, but he finally swung the ax mightily forward and smashed the god's stone face across the cheek.

Christians in the crowd held their breath. Some of them covered their eyes, afraid of the con-

sequences. But as the great statue's cheek crumbled under the force of the ax, nothing happened. Encouraged, the crowd raced forward to pull,

Although the original statue was destroyed, smaller statues of Serapis still exist.

63

kick, and hurl themselves at the statue and surrounding temple. They used axes, swords, and any other weapons they could find.

The great Serapeum finally began to crumble before them. Several members of the crowd pulled the remains of the statue from its stone seat and dragged it away from the temple grounds and through the streets of Alexandria.

The mob shouted as they pulled the crumbling statue down the city streets. Crowds of Christians and pagans lined the streets—some cheering along with the mob, and some standing in awed silence. It was rumored that on that day, thousands of pagans renounced their own religion, shocked at the sight of a statue of their precious god being dragged through the streets. Most of them converted to Christianity after seeing how powerful the religion was.

This was the goal of the archbishop—converting pagans, which they thought Hypatia was, to Christianity. The goal was also to build the strength of the Christian church and eliminate the threat of the

The Ptolemaic Sphinx (left) and the Pillar of Pompey, which were located near the statue of Serapis, are two of the few landmarks from ancient Alexandria that still exist today.

competing religions. Theophilus encouraged his followers to drag the statue through the streets because he wanted all of Alexandria's pagans to see just how weak their supposed god was.

Following through on the emperor's orders that pagan symbols be used to help the poor, Theophilus plotted another plan that would humiliate pagans. At ceremonies in the city's central square, he publicly melted down the valuable metal of pagan statues and used it either to create Christian symbols to display in the churches or to give to the poor. He most likely ordered the destruction of all books found on the grounds of the Serapeum as well. Some historians say that he then moved on to the Museum and ordered the destruction of the temple, as well as all of the books in the library.

Theophilus had one more goal: He wanted to replace the celebrated Serapeum—long a symbol of the scientific exploration of Hypatia, Theon, and others—with an equally renowned Christian symbol. It took several more years, but he eventually achieved his goal.

On the site of the former pagan temple, he oversaw the construction of a church dedicated to St. John the Baptist, a famous Christian figure. Theophilus even claimed to have in his pos-

> *There are many stories about how Theophilus frightened hundreds of Alexandria's pagans into converting to Christianity. According to one source, the archbishop received permission from the emperor to build a Christian church on the site of an abandoned temple. He then displayed pagan artwork and statues taken from the temple in a way that mocked the pagan symbols. Outraged pagans began rioting in the streets and ended up losing a bloody battle with Christians.*

As written in the Bible, John the Baptist was a prophet who baptized Jesus in the Jordan River.

session several personal belongings of St. John. The archbishop considered this replacement of the temple of Serapis with the church to be one of his greatest accomplishments. He had personally contributed to advancing Christianity in Alexandria. ᐧ

Chapter

7 A RUTHLESS ARCHBISHOP

Hypatia was likely between 25 and 35 years old when Theophilus oversaw the destruction of the Serapeum in 391. It is not known exactly where she was on that fateful day. Hypatia herself likely did not worship Serapis or any of the pagan gods. She mostly believed in mathematical and scientific truth. In fact, she counted many high-ranking Christians among her students. But she still probably felt threatened by the violent display of Christian fervor. She understood that in the eyes of many Christians, mathematicians and pagans were both seen as threats to the Christian religion.

Nevertheless, it does not seem that Hypatia was personally harassed by Theophilus or his followers. She remained a highly desired teacher. Christian

Theophilus' nephew, Cyril, who came to power after his uncle, was increasingly ruthless toward pagans.

families continued to hire her to teach their sons. She was also an intensely popular public figure. At a time when very few women were even known outside of their immediate families, Hypatia was recognized all over Alexandria. She was the only woman wearing academic robes and a laurel crown. She delivered speeches on philosophical topics at lecture halls and theaters around Alexandria.

Her home was also well known as the place where she received her students. Impressively decorated

The stadium seating in the theaters throughout the ancient world allowed hundreds of people to attend public lectures.

chariots could be seen outside her door daily, picking up and dropping off her students.

It seems that Hypatia's life passed in this manner for decades. Theophilus remained Alexandria's archbishop until his death in 412. Although he continued his persecution of the pagans, he left Hypatia alone. One reason for this may have been her ongoing friendship with Synesius, her former student. He had gone on to become the bishop of Ptolemais (in what is now Libya). He was well-respected within the Christian church and ranked below Theophilus among church leaders.

Synesius was a prolific letter writer, and he kept up a lifetime of correspondence with Hypatia. From Africa, he continued to praise his former teacher to Theophilus and other influential members of the church, as well as to Hypatia herself. He likely also defended her whenever church members began to speak badly of her, thereby allowing her to live without threat in Alexandria. One of Hypatia's fellow Neoplatonist philosophers, Damascius, described public opinion of Hypatia in his book, *The Life of Isidore*: "The whole city rightly loved her and worshipped her in a remarkable way, but the rulers of the city from the first envied her."

In the year 412, Hypatia's relatively untroubled lifestyle began to change. When Theophilus died that year, his nephew Cyril became Alexandria's archbishop. Cyril had learned to have no tolerance for non-Christians from his uncle, and he came to power ready to banish paganism from Alexandria once and for all. But Cyril was hungrier for power than his uncle had been, making him even more eager to rid the city of non-Christians. In addition to pagans, he viewed Jewish people as a threat to his ambitions.

When Cyril became archbishop, the governor—the Roman emperor's representative in Alexandria—

Cyril was determined to rid Alexandria of all non-Christians.

was Orestes, who was also a student of Hypatia. Cyril resented Orestes' power and wanted it for himself. He began to assert his authority in matters such as property and money that were not under his control as archbishop. At first, mostly because of Synesius' friendship with Hypatia, Cyril left the esteemed mathematician alone. But when Bishop Synesius died around 413, Hypatia was left without a defender in the Christian church.

Cyril had two reasons to despise Hypatia. Not only was she a non-Christian, but she was also becoming closer friends with his rival, Orestes. Orestes was a Christian, but he was determined to keep church laws and other laws separate in Alexandria. He believed the archbishop should focus on leading the church. This made him a bitter opponent of Cyril, who wanted to be in control of both Alexandria's church and its political government.

Many people at the time, including Cyril, believed that Hypatia was the driving force behind Orestes' insistence that church and politics be kept separate. Orestes and Hypatia spent hours together not only as student and teacher, but also as friends. They were often seen walking the streets of Alexandria together, and the governor's chariot was frequently spotted waiting outside Hypatia's house.

The rivalry between Cyril and Orestes was felt throughout the city. Many of Alexandria's Christians

> *Much of what we know about Hypatia's story comes from the fifth-century church historian Socrates Scholasticus. He wrote the following about the public's views of the famous philosopher: "Envy arose against this woman. She happened to spend a great deal of time with Orestes, and that stirred up slander against her among people of the church, as if she were one who prevented Orestes from entering into friendship with the Bishop."*

sided with Cyril, and most of the city's Jews and pagans sided with Orestes. But many of the common people, including Christians and non-Christians, just wanted the bloodshed to stop. They wanted to see peace between the two leaders. While Hypatia enjoyed popularity with the ruling class, she was not so influential with the common people. They could not afford for their children to be her students, and they had little time for the intellectual and philosophical ideas she expressed. They had more pressing concerns, like keeping themselves and their families safe in an increasingly violent city.

Cyril realized that by turning popular opinion against Hypatia, he could win his battle with Orestes. He helped convince people that Hypatia was responsible for Orestes' continued fighting against the church's authority. He most likely spread rumors about Hypatia being involved with witchcraft, which, along with fortune-telling, remained linked with mathematics in many people's minds. It was not hard to make the public believe that Hypatia's interest in math and science was the same as black magic—a practice feared as evil by the public. John, the bishop of Nikiu, reflected many people's feelings when he described Hypatia as:

> *[A] female philosopher, a pagan named Hypatia, and she was devoted at all times to magic, astrolabes and instruments of music, and she beguiled many people through Satanic wiles. And the governor of the city honored her exceedingly; for she had beguiled him through her magic.*

Even if they did not believe that Hypatia was practicing witchcraft, many Alexandrians were willing to believe other stories they heard about the female philosopher. Cyril's followers described her as the main obstacle to a reconciliation between Orestes and Cyril. They said that she was teaching the governor to be anti-Christian. John of Nikiu reported that Hypatia convinced Orestes not to attend church, and that as their friendship developed, the governor began spending time with more and more pagans, even "receiving the unbelievers at his house."

Bishop John was offended by other behavior by the governor as well. He claimed that Orestes spent too much time watching plays at the theater. Like many Christians, the bishop believed that art or music should be for purposes of worship only. He told the story of a violent attack made by Orestes on a Christian one night when the governor was at the theater:

> *And on a certain day when [Orestes and other non-Christians, including many Jews] were making merry over a theatrical exhibition connected with dancers, the governor of the city published [a law] regarding the public exhibitions in the city of Alexandria: and all the inhabitants of the city had assembled there (in the theater). Now Cyril, who had been appointed [archbishop] after Theophilus, was eager to gain exact intelligence regarding this [law]. And there was a man named Hierax, a Christian possessing understanding and intelligence who used to mock the pagans but was a devoted [Christian]. But when the Jews saw him in the theater they cried out and said: "This man has not come with any good purpose, but only to provoke an uproar." And Orestes was displeased with the children of the holy church, and Hierax was seized and subjected to punishment publicly in the theater, although he was wholly guiltless.*

Many historians do not believe John's account of the attack on Hierax, but they do agree that some sort of attack spurred citywide riots between Jews and Christians. The mood of Alexandria became even more tense. Fights frequently broke out between

Jews and Christians. For at least a few months, the Jewish-Christian fighting was more intense than the battles between pagans and Christians. ❧

Chapter

8 TRAGIC ENDING

❦

In early 415, Alexandria seemed like a war zone, as street fights between Jews and Christians took place almost daily. It is hard to know who was actually fueling these battles because most of the reports we have today come from either pro-Christian or anti-Christian sources.

According to pro-Christian writers, Jews were launching violent attacks on unsuspecting Christians. But later, anti-Christian writers reported that Cyril and his followers were persecuting Jews and other non-Christians.

At one point, Cyril called a meeting with the leaders of the Jewish community and told them they would face serious consequences if they did not end their persecution of Christians.

Hypatia's interest in mathematics, along with Cyril's accusations that she practiced witchcraft, led Christians to believe that she was a pagan.

As John of Nikiu reported:

> *[Cyril] sent word to the Jews as fol-*
> *lows: "Cease your hostilities against the*
> *Christians." But they refused to hearken*
> *to what they heard; for they gloried in*
> *the support of the [governor] who was*
> *with them, and so they added outrage to*
> *outrage and plotted a massacre through a*
> *treacherous device.*

Hearing the message from Cyril, many people in Alexandria's Jewish community became even angrier. One group of Jews came up with a plan to get back at their persecutors. In the middle of the night, the group ran through the streets calling out that the great Christian church of St. Alexander was on fire. Upon hearing this alarm, Christians rushed out of their houses in their nightclothes to save their church. Dashing into the darkened church, they saw no signs of fire, and they did not smell any smoke. Suddenly, they heard the shouts of an angry mob of Jews. The mob rushed into the church and attacked the startled Christians. Many Christians were killed.

Cyril was outraged, and he ordered Christians to retaliate against the Jews. A mob of Christians rushed into the city's Jewish area, surrounding their houses of worship. As many frightened Jews fled the city, Christians ransacked the synagogues. They grabbed sacred ornaments and destroyed them. In some

A floor mosaic from an Alexandrian church

synagogues, they sprinkled holy water and held ceremonies, claiming the buildings as Christian churches.

In the aftermath of this violence, Cyril issued an order that all Jews had to leave Alexandria. The archbishop's order infuriated the governor. Although Orestes was Christian, he vowed to stop the persecution of non-Christians. Orestes had control of Alexandria's official Roman Empire soldiers, and Cyril had his own army of 500 monks.

Roman soldiers stationed near Alexandria were under Orestes' command.

One day in 415, Cyril's army, led by a monk named Ammonius, attempted to kill Orestes. They rushed him, attacking him with swords and large stones. One of the stones Ammonius threw wounded the governor. As the governor stood bleeding, many of his bodyguards ran off, afraid for their lives. However, a throng of bystanders jumped to Orestes' defense. The group that saved the governor was made up of Christians who did not agree with the radical ideas of Cyril. Because of their assistance, the governor survived the assassination plot. He even captured

Ammonius and ordered that the monk be tortured and killed for his crime. Orestes' army carried out the order. This enraged Cyril. He managed to get Ammonius' body and then presided over a church ceremony making Ammonius a Christian saint.

In the midst of this violence and public rioting, Hypatia's life became endangered. Cyril's ongoing efforts to spread rumors about her involvement in witchcraft made the general public suspicious of her. As more and more people died in the city's religious riots, the public was ready to believe that one person was responsible for the bloodshed. By removing that person from the city forever, they believed they could rid Alexandria of violence.

The exact details of Hypatia's death are unclear, but historians are certain that she was murdered by a mob of Christians. Most accounts of the incident agree that she had been riding through the city streets when she was attacked and dragged from her chariot. They differ, though, on the method of her killing. According to one story, she was dragged into the church Caesarion and stabbed to death with pottery shards. According to another narrative, she was dragged through the city streets until she died. Still others say she was burned to death. Some

> The name of the church in which Hypatia was supposedly murdered, Caesarion, means "little Caesar" in Greek. It was also the name of Cleopatra and Julius Caesar's son.

Christians believe that in the minutes before her death in the church, Hypatia converted to Christianity. In any event, her death was sudden and violent.

How much Cyril was involved with Hypatia's death is unknown. Most historians agree that he helped to stir up anger and witchcraft suspicions about the philosopher. Some say that he personally ordered her murder. Some people say a man named Peter the Reader was the ringleader of the attack, and that he may have been working under Cyril's orders. Other than the name Peter the Reader, nothing is known about this alleged attacker.

Regardless of whether Cyril was responsible for Hypatia's murder, he was not immediately accused. Instead he seemed to have achieved his goal of increasing his power over Alexandria. Many residents of the city felt that Hypatia's death would serve as a warning to other close friends and followers of the governor. There are few reports of violence between Christians and non-Christians after the murder. Orestes most likely left the city after Hypatia's death, either in fear for his own life or in disgust over the act. He was no longer mentioned in historical accounts.

Christian supporters of Cyril viewed the murder of Hypatia—who was seen as a pagan and a witch—as a necessary deed. They felt it would further the cause of Christianity. As John of Nikiu reports: "And

all the people surrounded … Cyril and named him 'the new Theophilus'; for he had destroyed the last remains of idolatry in the city."

It seems that Cyril was successful not just in convincing Alexandrians that the murder was justified, but also in convincing the higher authorities of the Roman Empire. These leaders had the right to punish the archbishop for criminal activities, but they remained silent through 415. Cyril enjoyed a strengthened leadership role in Alexandria.

After Hypatia's death, the fighting in Alexandria decreased significantly.

Cyril lived until 444 and was later made a saint by the Roman Catholic Church.

Nearly 18 months after the murder, however, Cyril did receive consequences from the Roman Empire. In October 416, the emperor stripped Cyril of his authority over a group of soldiers known as parabolans. These 800 young men worked for the Alexandrian church. They collected ill, disabled, and homeless residents and carried them to hospitals or other places where they could be cared for.

For decades, the parabolans had reported to the archbishop, who often used them as a private army. It had most likely been parabolans who assisted the former archbishop, Theophilus, with the destruction of the Serapeum and other pagan temples. Parabolans almost certainly participated in the attack on Alexandria's Jewish quarters in 414 as well. Many people believe that it was this army of the archbishop that led the mob murder of Hypatia in the spring of 415.

Therefore, the emperor's order to remove the parabolans from the archbishop's control was a direct message that the emperor disapproved of these actions. The order reduced the number of parabolans from 800 to 500, and it placed them under the authority of the governor. However, the punishment lasted for only two years. By 418, Cyril had regained his authority over the parabolans, and he continued to have authority over Alexandria for more than 25 years. ℘

9 A Philosopher's Legacy

❦

Hypatia is considered one of the greatest female mathematicians and philosophers of all time. Yet few facts about her life are known. Much that is known about her—that she lived in Alexandria, that she was loved and respected as a teacher, and that she was violently murdered—comes from a few brief mentions in histories written by people who lived at the same time she did. Very few public records with biographical details exist from the late fourth century.

But even considering that she lived more than 1,500 years ago, the lack of information about such a famous person's life is remarkable. Several of her contemporaries—people who lived at the same time she did—reported that she wrote and edited several

A figurine of Hypatia was created to honor the Greek mathematician and philosopher.

textbooks and gave many speeches. Yet no copies of her work have survived. Although most accounts of Alexandrian history of the late fourth and early fifth centuries mention Hypatia, the authors never quite agree on the details of her life and death.

Some current historians believe there was a cover-up of Hypatia's murder by people who thought it reflected badly on the early Christian church. These historians believe that the early church censored many historical records and books of the time in order to hide ideas and facts that went against church thinking. One popular method was to "revise" books by changing the words when they were being hand-copied (the way literary works were preserved then).

One of Hypatia's best-known students, Synesius, wrote in a letter to his former teacher that he had been accused of storing unrevised copies of books in his library. Books carrying messages that were unpopular with church or political leaders were also frequently burned or destroyed. It is likely that many books written either by or about Hypatia were destroyed or altered shortly after her death.

The accounts of Hypatia's life that have survived tend to either accuse Cyril of Hypatia's murder or defend him. Cyril's accusers viewed him as ruthless and power-hungry, and some of them claim that he personally ordered Hypatia's killing. Cyril's defenders state that he had nothing to do with the attack. Some defenders of the early Roman Catholic Church—simply called the Christian church in Hypatia's day— argue that Cyril was not involved in the killing or the planning of the murder. Instead, writers such as Bishop John of Nikiu justify the murder by describing Hypatia as a witch who needed to be killed for the common good.

Despite attempts to revise or cover up the details of Hypatia's life and death, the story has kept its appeal throughout the centuries. Writers of history books, novels, and poems have embellished on the known details to create a legacy that is partly fact and partly fiction. Some of the more famous examples were written by the 18th-century French philosopher Voltaire and the 19th-century French poet Charles Leconte de Lisle. Both authors described Hypatia as a beautiful young woman—she was probably between 45 and 65 years old when she died—whose murder was planned by Cyril and the Christian church.

Charles Leconte de Lisle (1818–1894)

Charles Kingsley (1819–1875) urged the Church of England to help in easing social problems.

Also during the 1800s, British author Charles Kingsley wrote a novel called *Hypatia, Or the New Foes with an Old Face,* in which he describes the philosopher as young and beautiful at the time of her murder by a Christian mob under the orders of

Cyril. Kingsley was an Anglican clergyman who was strongly opposed to the Roman Catholic church.

By the mid-1800s, many writers depicted Hypatia's murder as an attempt by the Catholic church to squelch scientific thinking. In the words of American scientist J.W. Draper, Hypatia was a "valiant defender of science against religion." Since then, several fictionalized versions of her story have kept this opinion popular. In these novels, paganism is often associated with scientific learning, and Hypatia is usually the victim of Christian persecution.

While many of the known facts of Hypatia's life and death support these opinions, other facts make it hard to believe that she was killed for religious reasons. Hypatia was not religious herself. She knew many pagans and was familiar with the Greek pagan traditions. But she was not among the Alexandrians who tried to protect the Serapeum or other pagan temples from destruction. She probably had more Christians than pagans among her students. Her close friendships with many prominent Christians prevented Cyril from being able to directly attack her as a pagan. Instead, he

French poet Charles Leconte de Lisle described Hypatia as embodying physical beauty and the soul's immortality:

She alone survives,
immutable, eternal;
Death can scatter the
trembling universes
But Beauty still dazzles
with her fire,
and all is reborn in her,
And the worlds are still
prostrate beneath her
white feet!

and his followers spread rumors that she practiced witchcraft—something more feared than paganism, but also harder to prove. Regardless of what led to her murder, the brilliant philosopher was considered an intellectual threat by the archbishop.

More recently, women in Europe and North America have identified with Hypatia. Feminists admire her as a pioneering woman who broke free of society's restrictions on women in order to pursue her own intellectual interests. Two feminist magazines—one published at Michigan State University and the other in Athens, Greece—are called *Hypatia*. The university's *Hypatia*, which is subtitled *A Journal of Feminist Philosophy*, notes that it is named in honor of Hypatia as a reminder that "although many of us are the first women philosophers in our schools, we are not, after all, the first in history." In addition, the feminist artist Judy Chicago included Hypatia in a mixed-media sculpture of a dinner party of famous women throughout history.

The few extraordinary details of Hypatia's life have gone through a variety of interpretations, but most scholars agree on a few key points. She possessed great knowledge in the emerging fields of science, math, and philosophy. She dedicated her life to the pursuit of knowledge at a time when much of the world was embracing early Christianity and overlooking scientific truth in favor of religious beliefs.

As a female pioneer in mathematics, Hypatia inspired the creation of two feminist magazines.

HYPATIA

A Journal of Feminist Philosophy

SPECIAL ISSUE
Democratic Theory

EDITED BY
Noëlle McAfee and R. Claire Snyder

Volume 22 | Number 4 | Fall 2007

And as an independent female mathematician and philosopher during a time when women were discouraged from public life, her unyielding and persistent nature continues to be a shining example for women today. ℘

Life and Times

HYPATIA'S LIFE

c. 370-375

Hypatia possibly went to Athens to study

350

Earliest estimated birth date of Hypatia

350 A.D.

352

First definite date Christmas is celebrated on December 25

350

The city of Anbar, in present-day Iraq, is founded

370

Huns invade Europe and build a huge empire during the next 70 years

WORLD EVENTS

379

Theodosius becomes emperor of the Roman Empire, including Alexandria

385

Theophilus becomes archbishop of Alexandria

385

383

St. Jerome's Latin translation of the Bible, the Vulgate, is published

387

St. Patrick, who introduced Christianity to Ireland, is born in Scotland

HYPATIA'S LIFE

391

Serapeum is destroyed and converted to a Christian church

389

Theodosius issues laws turning all the major pagan holidays into workdays

385

404

Last gladiator competition takes place in Rome

400

Use of iron spreads through eastern Africa

WORLD EVENTS

c. 405

Hypatia's father, Theon, dies

412

Theophilus dies and his nephew Cyril becomes Alexandria's archbishop

406

Stained glass is used for the first time in Roman churches

410

Visigoths overrun Rome, symbolizing the end of the western Roman Empire

412

Proclus, patriarch of Constantinople, is born; best known for his defense of Mary as the mother of God against some early Christians who objected to the title

HYPATIA'S LIFE

413

Synesius, Hypatia's former student and influential Christian friend, dies

414

Power struggle between Archbishop Cyril and Governor Orestes intensifies; Cyril plots to assassinate Orestes

414

Ataulf, king of the Visigoths, marries his Roman captive, Galla Placidia; her mausoleum in Ravenna, Italy, was named a U.N. world heritage site in 1996

WORLD EVENTS

415

Hypatia is murdered by
a mob in Alexandria

416

Roman poet Rutilius Claudius
Namatianus writes of his
journey from Rome to his
native Gaul; fragments of the
two-book poem survive and
shed light on fifth-century life

DATE OF BIRTH: Estimated between 350 and 370

BIRTHPLACE: Alexandria, in the Roman Empire (present-day Egypt)

FATHER: Theon (c. 330–405)

MOTHER: Unknown

EDUCATION: Educated by her father, Theon, probably at Alexandria's Museum

DATE OF DEATH: March 415

PLACE OF BURIAL: Unknown

Further Reading

Adams, Michelle Medlock. *The Life and Times of Cleopatra.* Hockessin, Del.: Mitchell Lane Publishers, 2005.

Lassieur, Allison. *The Ancient Greeks*. New York: Franklin Watts, 2004.

Nardo, Don. *The Fall of the Roman Empire*. Farmington Hills, Mich.: Lucent Books, 2004.

Trumble, Kelly. *The Library of Alexandria*. New York: Clarion Books, 2003.

Look for more Signature Lives books about this era:

Alexander the Great: *World Conqueror*

Aristotle: *Philosopher, Teacher, and Scientist*

Socrates: *Ancient Greek in Search of Truth*

Thucydides: *Ancient Greek Historian*

ON THE WEB

For more information on this topic,
use FactHound.

1. Go to *www.facthound.com*
2. Type in this book ID: 0756537606
3. Click on the *Fetch It* button.

FactHound will find the best
Web sites for you.

HISTORIC SITES

National Archaeological
Museum of Athens
44 Patission St.
106 82 Athens
Attica, Greece
011-30-210-8217724
Greek art, including sculpture, pottery,
bronzes, and prehistoric items

The Metropolitan Museum of Art
1000 Fifth Ave.
New York, NY 10028
212/535-7710
Artifacts, statues, and literature from
ancient Greece

astronomy
scientific study of the universe, especially of the motion, position, size, composition, and behavior of stars, planets, and other heavenly bodies

Athena
Greek goddess of wisdom

authority
right to do something or to tell other people what to do

chariot
two-wheeled, horse-drawn vehicle used in ancient times, often without seats

dialectic
teaching method using question-and-answer sessions between the teacher and the students to obtain knowledge

eclipse
when one object in space blocks light and keeps it from shining on another object in space

feminists
people who support equal rights for women in all parts of society

heretical
term to describe beliefs that contradict established religious teaching

intellectual
person who spends most of his or her time thinking and studying

Muses
goddesses in Greek mythology that preside over song, poetry, arts, and science

Neoplatonists
people who believe in a philosophical system that
combines Plato's beliefs with some Jewish and Christian
ideas, especially the belief that there is one source for
all existence

omnipotent
all-powerful; often used in reference to a higher being

omniscient
all-knowing; often used in reference to a higher being

pagan
a term often used to describe a person who does not
believe in the Christian, Jewish, or Islamic God

papyrus
paperlike material created from the papyrus plant; it was
made into scrolls and used in ancient times

persecuted
continually treated cruelly or unfairly, especially because
of ideas or political beliefs

philosophy
the study of truth, wisdom, the nature of reality,
and knowledge

prominent
famous or important

Ptolemaic
relating to the ideas of the second-century geographer
Ptolemy, such as the view that Earth is at the center of
the universe; Ptolemaic Empire refers to the family that
ruled Egypt for 300 years

Trinity
Christian concept of three persons—Father, Son, and Holy
Spirit—united as one God

Chapter 3:

Page 31, line 13: Socrates Scholasticus. "The Martyrdom of the Pagan Philosopher Hypatia. Alexandria, 415 A.D." *Ecclesiastical History VII.15.* 27 March 2007. www.stoa.org/diotima/anthology/wlgr/wlgr-religion451.shtml

Page 31, line 26: Michael A.B. Deakin. "Hypatia and Her Mathematics." *The American Mathematical Monthly* 101.3 (March 1994): 234–243. 2 April 2007. www.maa.org/pubs/calc_articles.html, p. 238.

Page 35, line 4: "The Martyrdom of the Pagan Philosopher Hypatia. Alexandria, 415 A.D."

Page 35, lines 12 and 23: Ibid.

Chapter 4:

Page 43, line 1: "Hypatia of Alexandria." *The New Banner Institute, Inc.* 5 May 2007. www.newbanner.com/AboutPic/athena/raphael/nbi_hypa.html

Page 43, line 13 and sidebar: Ibid.

Page 45, line 6: Sameh M. Arab. "Bibliotheca Alexandrina: A History of the Library of Alexandria." *Arab World Books.* 22 March 2007. www.arabworld-books.com/bibliothecaAlexandrina.htm

Chapter 5:

Page 48, line 12: "Hypatia of Alexandria."

Page 50, line 27: Ibid.

Page 52, line 22: Ibid.

Page 53, line 2: Ibid.

Chapter 7:

Page 71, line 23: "Damascius: The Life of Hypatia from the Suda." Trans. Jeremiah Reedy. 1993. 14 April 2007. http://cosmopolis.com/alexandria/hypatia-bio-suda.html

Page 74, sidebar: Maria Dzielska. *Hypatia of Alexandria.* Trans. F. Lyra. Cambridge, Mass.: Harvard University Press, 1995, p. 19.

Page 75, line 4: "John of Nikiu: The Life of Hypatia." *Chronicle* 84.87–103. 12 May 2007. www.cosmopolis.com/alexandria/hypatia-bio-john.html

Page 75, line 21: Ibid.

Page 76, line 3: Ibid.

Chapter 8:

Page 80, line 2: Ibid.

Page 84, line 28: Ibid.

Chapter 9:

Page 93, line 6: *Hypatia of Alexandria,* p. 11.

Page 93, sidebar: *Hypatia of Alexandria,* p. 5.

Page 94, line 15: "Hypatia: A Journal of Feminist Philosophy." *Hypatia.* 23 April 2007. www.msu.edu/~hypatia/

Arab, Sameh M. "Bibliotheca Alexandrina: A History of the Library of Alexandria." *Arab World Books.* 22 March 2007. www.arabworldbooks.com/bibliothecaAlexandrina.htm

"Damascius: The Life of Hypatia From the Suda." Trans. Jeremiah Reedy. 1993. 14 April 2007. http://cosmopolis.com/alexandria/hypatia-bio-suda.html

Deakin, Michael A.B. "Hypatia and Her Mathematics." *The American Mathematical Monthly* 101.3 (March 1994): 234–243. 2 April 2007. www.maa.org/pubs/calc_articles.html

Dzielska, Maria. *Hypatia of Alexandria.* Trans. F. Lyra. Cambridge, Mass.: Harvard University Press, 1995.

"Hypatia: A Journal of Feminist Philosophy." *Hypatia.* 23 April 2007. www.msu.edu/~hypatia/

"Hypatia of Alexandria." *Astronomy & Space: From the Big Bang to the Big Crunch.* 3 vols. Farmington Hills, Mich.: Thomson Gale, 2007. 19 April 2007. http://galenet.galegroup.com/servlet/BioRC

"Hypatia of Alexandria." *Math & Mathematicians: The History of Math Discoveries Around the World.* 2 vols. Farmington Hills, Mich.: Thomson Gale, 2007. 17 April 2007. http://galenet.galegroup.com/servlet/BioRC

"Hypatia of Alexandria." *The New Banner Institute, Inc.* 5 May 2007. www.newbanner.com/AboutPic/athena/raphael/nbi_hypa.html

"Hypatia of Alexandria." *Notable Mathematicians.* Farmington Hills, Mich.: Thomson Gale, 2007. 23 April 2007. http://galenet.galegroup.com/servlet/BioRC

"John of Nikiu: The Life of Hypatia." *Chronicle* 84.87–103. 12 May 2007. www.cosmopolis.com/alexandria/hypatia-bio-john.html

Krasner-Khait, Barbara. "Survivor: The History of the Library." *History Magazine* October/November 2001. 12 March 2007. www.history-magazine.com/libraries.html

Rist, J.M. "Hypatia." *Phoenix* Autumn 1965: 214–225.

Rowlandson, J., ed. *Women and Society in Greek and Roman Egypt.* Cambridge: Cambridge University Press, 1998.

Scholasticus, Socrates. "The Martyrdom of the Pagan Philosopher Hypatia. Alexandria, 415 A.D." *Ecclesiastical History VII.15.* 27 March 2007. www.stoa.org/diotima/anthology/wlgr/wlgr-religion451.shtml

Waithe, Mary Ellen. "Finding Bits and Pieces of Hypatia." *Hypatia's Daughters: Fifteen Hundred Years of Women Philosophers.* Ed. Linda Lopez McAlister. Bloomington: Indiana University Press, 1996.

Sandy Donovan has written several books for young readers about history, economics, government, and other topics. She has also worked as a newspaper reporter, a magazine editor, and a Web site developer. She has a bachelor's degree in journalism and a master's degree in public policy, and lives in Minneapolis, Minnesota, with her husband and two sons.

Image Credits